FREDERICK

The Greatest Goodness of God
Are we Free?

Volume II of the series Living Love

first edition

author's edition

April/2021

Maringá - PR

ISBN: 978-65-00-20661-6 (digital version):
ISBN: 978-65-00-20663-0 (physical version):

I dedicate this work to Dr. Paulo Nassar Frange, a person of fine lineage and a doctor of extraordinary value, whose advice I carry throughout my life.

Summary

As he returned on his way, someone ran and knelt before him, asking, "Good Master, what shall I do to inherit eternal life?" Jesus answered: Why do you call me good? No one is good but God.

BJ, Mk 10:17-18

1.   Introducing

I start this book in a different way: instead of instigating the reader's curiosity, I already answer - from the outset - what is the greatest gift from the goodness of God and position myself on the subject, to then also talk about related topics: human responsibility and divine sovereignty.

There is no way to speak of human freedom dissociated from human responsibility and divine sovereignty, for these belong to the context of that. In this work, I examine if there are any consequences of our actions and to what extent divine interference occurs in events and in our acts. The extent to which we can speak of human freedom in the face of divine sovereignty and the possible punishments we may receive for our merciless acts.

This format that I adopt - to reveal, in advance, the target of this study, does not aim to discourage reading; on the contrary, it allows the reader to place himself at every moment, without taking away from him the right to reach his own conclusions. The reader, of course, will not be content with a diagnosis without all the means that led to this understanding being presented in a complete and rational way, which I hope to do throughout this book.

I choose, once again, to adopt a direct and clear language, fleeing from the far-fetched approach so to the liking of some who incur in the obscurity of their works.

When you, the reader, find the Hebrew word **"Iahweh" (reads** Jehovah), it will mean the one God. When I wanted to refer to these names simply or I designate Jesus Christ also as Nazarene, Son Sent, Only Begotten Son, Jesus of Nazareth. to the Holy Spirit or to Jesus Christ in this work,

To systematize everything I have proposed to write about divine love, I deal with the theme in the series "living love", composed of the following independent books (but complementary and harmonic):

The Conditional Love (in) of God" (1st book in 2 parts);

"The Greatest Goodness of God" (2nd book);

"The providence and love of God" (Book 3).

In this volume, in order for the reader to have the **biblical** text at hand, whether for consultation or confrontation, I also made a point of quoting ipsis from the biblical passages that support the arguments, sometimes incorporating them in the main text, Now citing them in the end notes for the Jerusalem Bible, that Brief "BJ", but also used the New International Bible Version (BNVI), the Ecumenical Bible Translation (BTE), the Jewish Complete Bible (BCJ) and the Bible of the Worker - Almeida Revised and Updated (BO). do not interrupt the reasoning there developed. For that, I used

I also use the "New Testament Interlinear", which brings the Greek text alongside the Portuguese translation of João Ferreira de Almeida, which abrevio as "NTI".

I am aware that I also write for atheists, Jews and people of non-Christian religions. I have tried to give both of them "a rational answer to everyone who asks for an explanation of the hope" that is in Christianity and, of course, in me also with regard to the faith I place in Jesus Christ. [1]

And I do so as a minister of the Gospel, of those who have the wounds of Christ, and who live this same Gospel in dependence and guidance of God, animated by the Holy Spirit and living in the grace of Jesus Christ, because I have been plucked from perdition and am today enjoying the abundant life bestowed by the Heavenly Council.

I consider myself fortunate if you, the reader, approach the love bestowed by the Heavenly Council, formed by Jehovah, the Holy Spirit, and Jesus Christ, and recognize the sovereignty of God in your life.

This work comes to be the result of divine revelation received by me, who came to shed light on the study of the Bible, always guided by the Holy Spirit.

First and foremost, this work was formulated for the honor and glory of the one and only Jehovah!

2. The Exponent of God's Goodness

As we approach in our book "The Love (In)Conditional of God: first part", divine love is established within a relationship, while the goodness of God constitutes an impersonal and universal act, as, for example, the rain [2]*that* falls on everyone and the sun that rises for the just and unjust.

But what is the greatest manifestation of God's goodness?

We can think about life or the breath of life. But this gift is inherent in the formation of the human being and represents what he is. It is an extraordinary gift for the constitution of being, but it was not given after human formation, but in an act coinciding with it.

Returning to the question, when I formulated it for myself, the answer came immediately: the sending of Jesus Christ. whereas, however, it was an offshoot of Jesus' mission and consistent in the salvation of all who believe through the new birth, I classify it (sending) as an act of love, the purpose of which was to inaugurate a relationship with humanity, and not just as a kind act in the strict sense.

Continuing in my evaluation, I began to consider the freedom of the human being as a fundamental gift without equal on the part of God that reaches the whole of Humanity.

It is a fundamental gift because, were it not for the freedom that God granted, it would not have made sense to "send Jesus" for the salvation of all those who accepted Him as Lord and Savior.

In advancing the conclusion of this book, I hope not to discourage you from reading the rest of the book; On the contrary, this increases my responsibility to refute, at every step, in a complete and reasoned manner, the objections that other great theologians have made on the subject.

As an alternative to human freedom, God could have created an intelligent being, but with superior instincts and necessarily obedient to God.

If God had preferred this option, there would be no freedom and consequently no regeneration by the Holy Spirit, nor sending Jesus Christ into the world for salvation.

Instinctive beings would not need to be saved, because sin would not be a valid option for them.

The freedom of the human being is the exponent of God's goodness, greater than the sending of the Son to salvation, because there would be no "sending" without human freedom.

God has the bestowal of freedom in high esteem, so much so that angels are likewise endowed with liberty for their actions, and there was room for the heavenly rebellion of Lucifer,

who commanded 1/3 of the angels.

3. How to Understand Human Freedom

What is freedom anyway? Are we human beings free?

Life is a succession of choices: what we will study; where we will graduate; who we're going to marry. Even to define the flavor of the ice cream we will taste, we need to make a choice.

But are these choices free? Do we choose with complete independence, or are we influenced, or even governed by external elements?

These questions have challenged religious and philosophers of all ages, who have addressed different explanations and consequences of the presence or absence of freedom in decision-making.

According to the Wikipédia, freedom is the ability to act on its own, with self-determination. The philosopher Schopenhauer defines freedom as the power of acting by distinguishing it from the will, which he conceptualizes as the power of will.

For determinism, the human being is not free, because all the acts practiced would be caused by previous facts, concluding this aspect that the human being cannot be held responsible for his actions.

For the German philosopher Artur Schopenhauer (1788-1860), the free word means what is not necessary under any relationship, which is not determined for any reason or reason, because, if this happens, the act is not free, but constrained by a need.

Free will is treated by philosophy of religion in a particular way, because it contains special elements such as sin, God's intervention, and responsibility in the final judgment.

For this philosophy of religion, or theology, human freedom is intertwined with theodicy, which is the set of arguments that seek to reconcile the presence of evil in the world before the belief of the supreme goodness and omnipotence of God.

Is the current questions among scholars why God permits evil, being exceedingly omnipotent and kind? In creating the human being, who does evil, would God have created or been responsible for the evil that exists in the world?

To answer this, the Bishop of Hippo, Saint Augustine, who lived from 354 to 430 A.D., maintained that the source of evil is man himself, who received the ability to decide freely and choose evil, evil being the absence of God. Sin, for him, results from the misuse of free will, being free will a good thing in itself. As was the divine creation of human eyes, which was a good thing, which did not prevent human beings from misusing their sight through covetousness and lust.

For Saint Augustine, man's free will was weakened by concupiscence, that is, by the passions of body and soul inherited by original sin.

The doctrine of Bishop Augustine of Hippo had an evident weakness. The notion of free will focused only on freedom without associating it with responsibility, which would be as a side effect not participating in the concept.

But if men are free moral agents, one can argue whether it follows that they would have freedom to sin. Would God, then, consent to sin?

To circumvent this, St.Augustine made a distinction between free will and freedom. God gave free will to man, but only the human being who does not sin has freedom. Freedom is the good use of free will. The misuse of free will is the result of man's inclination to original sin.

Another important philosopher who presented a valid philosophical explanation to solve the question of freedom, excluding from it the power to sin, was St.Anselm of Canterbury (1033-1109). He argues that a will incapable of sinning presents itself freer than a will capable of sinning. He argues, then, that one thing that diminishes the freedom of the will when it is added to the will, cannot be freedom, nor part of it.

The monk Pelagius of Brittany, who lived from 350 to 423 AD, a contemporary of Augustine of Hippo, maintained that man is born good and sins by imitation, and can have a sinless life with his natural gifts.

For him, corruption would not have been passed down hereditarily to the descendants of Adam. Adam would have been a bad example, while Christ would have been a good example. Grace would be a facilitating element for obedience, but not necessary for salvation.

But Sephardpelagianism, whose main theologian was John Cassian, a monk of Marseilles in France, argued that the human being receives salvation exclusively from God through grace, but is dependent on human initiative, of good will toward God. For him, man needs to take the first step toward God and God completes the process.

The discussion was again intensified in the 16th century with contemporaries Erasmus of Rotterdam and Martin Luther, the former affirming and the latter denying the existence of free will.

Erasmus of Rotterdam uses a powerful argument in favor of his thesis, namely that man could not be blamed for the practice of sins if he did not have the freedom to decide between good and evil, having that Scholar defined free will as the "force of human will by which the human being can apply himself to the things that lead to eternal salvation or turn away from them".

Erasmus considered that opting for God's ways implied human co-participation (effort and will) in conjunction with God's action, forming a synergy.

Conversely, Luther denies the existence of the free will of the human being, calling the decision-making process servant-will. To him, either man is a servant of Satan, or of God, whether or not he has received divine grace.

For Luther, it is not possible for man to perform any work to save himself, for he has the depraved and fallen nature, without free will, being captive, subject and servant to the will of God or Satan.

Luther also defended the foreknowledge of God and his sovereignty: everything that happens to man is the fruit of the irresistible sovereignty of God, for God not only knows, but also makes and controls everything and everyone.

It is quite useful, for the study, the differentiation between freedom and free will. Schopenhauer, in his work: "Free will", defines freedom as the power of acting and the will as the power of willing.

There are three stages of human action: thought, will, and realization. Thought aggregates all information, knowledge, the memory of previous facts. Then you follow the will, the will, or the desire of the person. Finally, the mind makes a choice and executes it, that is, performs the chosen action.

Paul of Tarsus taught that the sinner wants to do good (will), but cannot do it, and is therefore not free. This, however, cannot be generalised: there are people who wish to do evil and do so. It is only the constrained sinner who presents non-conformity between the will and the accomplishment of the action, and who can repent.

Perhaps it was this sense of dissatisfaction between the will and the action, which explains the words of the Nazarene, that we can be truly free, by the fact that the constrained sinner does not like to sin and, after conversion, he does the good that his will desires to do, being completely free, as will also be completely free the assumed sinner who wishes to do evil and practices it without resentment on the assumption that assumes responsibility for his actions.

Returning to the question, "If God has given us freedom, are we free to sin?" the answer is flatly negative. We can logically extract this answer from two sentences with their 3 logical premises:

> First Sentence
>
> First premise: It is human nature to do good deeds for yourself and others.

Premise 2: Human will does not wish to act against its nature.

3rd) The Human Being is free only when he practices his own actions of his nature.

Second Sentence

First premise: The nature of the Human Being is good.

Second premise: The Human Being violence his nature when he practices evil.

 Third premise: The Human Being is only free when he does good.

I am not saying that human beings have not been affected by original sin.

I agree with this and believe that man is inclined toward evil and relate this characteristic as an antecedent that influences the will.

But the human being is also influenced by another antecedent, which is his conscience and scruples that give him the right direction to follow.

My goal is to demonstrate that these philosophical statements are consistent with the Scriptures, with the logic and with the experience of the empirical world.

4. Criticism of the Terminology "Free Will"

I consider the terminologies "free will" and "servant-will" to be criticized, which highlight the absence or presence of the element "freedom" of the human will.

This element, taken to any of its extremes, whether absolute freedom or absolute absence of freedom, would result in the moral irresponsibility of the human being.

Both freedom and servility in their absolute modalities remove God's justification for judging his creatures. We can illustrate this by the situation in which someone receives, from authority, a revolver with the permission to do with him what he pleases. This person decides to shoot someone else, and cannot be later censured by the authority that gave him the revolver. Thus, even if I do an act under irresistible duress, I cannot be found guilty by it.

What defines human will in a certain, invariable and absolute way is responsibility. The human being is responsible for his earthly decisions and will give an account of what he has accomplished even in a future time. Man's will was granted by God to measure his responsibility. For this reason, we suggest the expression "responsible will".

Will and responsibility will always exist absolutely, while freedom will always be limited and variable.

While we do not have an absolutely liberating earthly existence, we also do not have an absolute servile existence.

Erasmus of Rotterdam's objection to Luther's Serb-will is that one cannot blame a human being without a margin of freedom.

God allows us the will, not the free will, but the responsible one as read in the Scriptures:

> In the beginning God created man, and delivered him to his own judgment: And he gave him commandments and precepts.
>
> If thou wilt keep the commandments, and do always faithfully that which is acceptable to God, they shall keep thee.
>
> He has set water and fire before you: he stretches out his hand to whatever you desire.
>
> Life and death, good and evil are before man: whatever he chooses, it will be given to him.
>
> Ecclesiastes 15:14 to 18
>
> This day I call heaven and earth to witness against you, that I have set before you clearly the ways of life and death; the blessing and the curse. Choose therefore the way of life, that I may live fully, you and your seed.
>
> Deuteronomy 30:19

5.   The   Antecedent Elements

Background is all the elements that influence decisions. They are necessary or occasional.

Human will is associated with necessary antecedents, such as responsibility before God given by conscience and inclination to evil, and occasional antecedents such as regeneration, Mosaic law, and the beliefs and values received in secular life.

Every human being has been endowed by God with a conscience, that is, a knowledge of good and evil regardless of being Christian, Jew, any other religion, or atheist.

Whenever we are faced with a problem, consciousness causes our minds to evoke the beacons of what is just, lawful, good and constructive.

Simultaneously and moved by a force of direction contrary to consciousness, we have an inclination to do evil. This is the trend; the first negative reaction to an opportunity. Whenever we have a chance, and usually when we know we're going to get away with it, there's a good chance we'll do the wrong thing.

Even knowing the just and unjust, right and wrong, our first reaction is to consider strongly the practice of a bad action.

Next to the necessary, we'll find the occasional background. Regeneration is one of them. It strengthens consciousness and combats the inclination to evil. The Regenerated Man is the one who has a greater ability to resist the forces of evil and practice good things that are natural to him.

Another criticism that can be made especially to Luther and St.Augustine is that, for these theologians, only the regenerated are of God, remaining to the others eternal condemnation as sinners irremediably lost and servile to Satan, deprived of divine grace.

However, even the unconverted may be declared righteous in the Divine Tribunal provided they have acted in accordance with the consciousness that God has endowed all human beings. Of course, this hypothesis has a lower probability of happening, but it is not impossible.

Paul of Tarsus states that the Gentiles "who have no law, do by nature, according to the law, having no law, serve as the law for themselves. These show the standard of the law engraved in his heart" (Paul of Tarsus, BO, Rom 2:14-15).

I would like to talk a little more about the background. We can compare our mind to an intelligent computer. The antecedents are nothing more than the dice that were cast in our mind. Already the inclination for evil triggers human rebellion against God. It's almost a feeling.

All of these antecedents are originally neutral in our mind, or in the "hardware" of the computer, in the sense that they point in a direction, but are not decisive for our actions. But it's data that can turn into information when we add our own judgements to it.

What is a judgment? The Wikipédia defines it as a judgment on the correctness or incorrectness of something, or the usefulness of something, based on a personal point of view.

To issue a value judgment, each person assigns a moral, ethical, and instrumental value to neutral data in considering the object to be known and the situation surrounding it, to conclude, from his personal point of view, whether a thing is good, bad, useful, useless, existing or non-existent.

As only data, the antecedents are neutral records that do not influence decisively our will. It is only when we lend our judgements to the background that they influence the will.

So we can say that the antecedents we speak of, do not directly and decisively influence our freedom. Only after they receive the influx of value judgments is our will sensitized.

That is the reflection I would like to leave on the strength of our freedom of will. It is not an absolute freedom as we have seen, but certainly a powerful freedom that gives us the freedom to take sufficiently free decisions.

I would like to transcribe an article entitled "an argument in favor of free will", authored by General Harrison, in the work "The 100 most important arguments of Western philosophy".

> "However, there is an almost unanimous agreement that free will is necessary to establish moral responsibility. That is, free will is necessary to

make us worthy of praise, censorship, reward or punishment for our actions, and to make valid the so-called "reactive attitudes", such as resentment, guilt and forgiveness.

Just as it is widely accepted that moral responsibility requires free will, it is also widely accepted that we are morally responsible for at least part of what we do for part of the time."

Therefore, it is widely accepted to argue that human moral responsibility stems from his free will, or responsible will as I prefer to say.

6. How to Understand Human Responsibility

Human responsibility is closely associated with free will.

Always when we talk about free will, we are talking about responsibility and the reader will agree with this in the course of the study.

The Bible teaches that we will all be judged by the Heavenly Tribunal. John the Baptist preached, "The axe is laid at the root of the trees, and every tree that does not bear good fruit shall be cut down and cast into the fire" (Matthew 3:10). The Nazarene taught that "whosoever shall say 'mad' is in danger of going into the fire of hell" (Matthew 5:21)

I have also argued in previous lines that human will was, perhaps, mistakenly called free will, or servant-will by Luther, and that the more appropriate terminology would be "responsible will", regardless of the amount of freedom that will be used.

This is because freedom is something that happens in the moment immediately following the responsible-will, that is, it is not part of the concept of human will. That is not why it is less important, only that action, the freedom to act, or, as the German philosopher Artur Schopenhauer liked to say, the power of acting, is something that is outside the will, although it can relate to it.

First, I have the power of will, the will, the desire, or the will; One moment later I have the power to act, freedom.

For some philosophers, such as Schopenhauer, arbitrariness and freedom can be considered synonymous.

In reality, however, that is not the case. I might want to do good. The conscience - that God has endowed me, inclines me to it, but it is not in me to practice it and behold I realize the evil that I hate. This was well explained by Paul of Tarsus.

Therefore, arbitrariness and freedom are different things, not always coincident, so freedom is something secondary to arbitrariness. It's not always what I want to do that I do!

At this point it is important to clarify that the divine judgment reaches not only the action, but the thoughts, as Jesus of Nazareth taught when he said that the lust for a woman already constitutes adultery for man.

In this case, there is the will of the hypothetical man, but not the action.

Another point is that freedom cannot be absolute, nor totally removed from the human being. It cannot be absent and also cannot be 100% present.

Divine judgment would not be justified in either of these extreme hypotheses. Whether one considers that one has full freedom, or whether one considers that one has no freedom at all.

Now if freedom does not conceptually participate in the will, nor presents itself as something absolute, then it is mistaken to call the will "free will".

But why are we suggesting the expression will-responsible?

Because responsibility is part of the essence of will as a necessary antecedent.

Why do I say that?

Because liability is a necessary limitation of will. It functions as an antecedent cause of will. We have seen in previous lines that Schopenhauer argued that there is no absolute free will when it is determined for a reason or a reason.

So the commandments of God function as a motive for will, and it is a necessary motive, because no one will escape divine judgment, and the person can be rewarded or punished according to the limitation that will has received.

Therefore, responsibility functions as a limiter that is invariably present in human will.

It could be argued that we all have temporary absolute freedom during the time we mediate our earthly existence and judgment.

That, however, is not true. The second coming of Jesus is a sure thing (for those who believe so) and the timeliness of his return can be demonstrated. We can take a specific person who was born today. We will estimate that she will live to be 100 years old and we will agree that the second coming will occur the day she completes her 100th birthday. We know that she will not be surprised by the trial that took place that day, because the person was certain that it would take place. So we have to cross that day off, because the trial won't be a surprise to our hypothetical person. So, let's go back one day, it'll be the penultimate day of your life. On that penultimate day, the trial will have to take place and therefore it will come as no surprise to the person in question. So we must scratch the penultimate day of life and so on and so forth until we come to this day. Nor will it be a surprise today if Jesus of Nazareth returns.

Thus, it is shown that the second coming of the Nazarene can happen at this very moment and our will is limited by this necessary antecedent.

7. Human Responsibility and God's Sovereignty

Human moral responsibility is an inescapable reality for those who believe in the Bible and its foundation lies in human will.

How to understand divine sovereignty in the midst of human will? The Holy Scriptures contain many accounts of the divine acts intervening in events and in the human will.

This is also an inescapable biblical reality!

How to reconcile these two true and coexisting biblical records?

Starting from the premise that God was interfering in all everyday events and in Human History, should it be asked if Man could be held responsible for the acts practiced even if completely determined by God?

The answer would be logically negative, because if God intervened in everything and in everyone, determining all acts and events, there could be no moral responsibility for the Human Being, who would be a mere plaything in the powerful and completely sovereign hands of the Most High.

Likewise, if we were to admit that the Human Being was a completely liberated creature, there would be no room for his moral responsibility, because, in the hypothesis under consideration, he would receive a carte blanche from God to do as he pleased.

By virtue of these logical reasoning, we are forced to conclude that freedom is neither absent nor complete in the human being. But freedom is a sizable fraction of our will.

To talk about the tension between sovereignty and human will, which has challenged theology in these two thousand years, I would like to begin to address the sovereignty of God.

Someone has already said that discussions end when concepts are defined. I will begin by addressing the concept of sovereignty.

Sovereignty consists in the use of divine omnipotence arising from a decision of God's own, present, free and unilateral, to intervene in an event of history according to its good purposes.

It is not accurate to say that omnipotence consists in the divine ability to do all things. We must add the predicate "possible" to the things on which God can act. God, for example, cannot make a circle square-shaped.

We can also say that God does not invade the freedom of human will either. If that happened, sovereignty would erase the will.

Consider the following biblical passage in which Jesus exclaims, "Jerusalem, Jerusalem, you, who kills the prophets and stones those who are sent to you! How many times I wanted to reunite your children, how the chicken gathers its chicks under its wings, but you didn't want to. Behold, your house will be deserted" (Matthew 24:37-38).

We have here the will of God which has been frustrated by the human will. Many Jews in Jerusalem did not want Jesus to gather them. Although God wanted the conversion of Israel, most Jews rejected it.

This is because God has saved a margin of freedom in human will that is, at one time, responsible, and at the other, partially liberated.

At the risk of frustrating many people, God cannot see the future either. It's mathematically impossible to see the future.

God simply preordains the facts and events to achieve a certain result within His purpose.

I like to illustrate this by comparing God to an unbeatable chess player. He knows all the rules of the game, the value of each piece, the weaknesses of the opponent. He is the best international chess player of all time.

What does God do, the unstoppable chess player?

He can predict accurately, for example, that he will checkmate against the opponent in a certain number of moves.

Anyone who knows chess knows that this is perfectly feasible.

When the player predicts checkmate, he does so on the premise that the opponent will not be able to stop checkmate even if he plays the best possible.

The checkmate announced by the unbeatable player is inevitable regardless of the opponent's responses.

God, as an unbeatable chess player, always has the initiative of the game.

What is the game initiative?

The game initiative is an indispensable strategy to win games that allows one of the players to impose their game and order both their pieces and influence the positioning of the opponent's pieces on the board according to their goals in the game. While the player holds the initiative, he can always execute his attack plan and have the time of the match in his favor, causing the opponent to be forced to defend himself within the game plan of those who have the initiative, that is, the opponent cannot put into practice a plan of attack and, at the same time, he forces himself to move his pieces only defensively, because he is under heavy fire. Meanwhile, the player with initiative is imposing his game and has the time of the match in his favor.

God is this unique, unbeatable chess player who takes the initiative of the game.

Thus, there is no talk that God sees the future. God uses mathematical probabilities to plan and predict his actions.

Returning to the subject of sovereignty and analyzing the biblical accounts, we identify the first relevant and invariable aspect: that divine sovereignty is localized.

Sovereignty is located in terms of places, peoples, and people, which are in God's purpose.

In the time of the Old Testament, the main focus of God's work was the Hebrews, the people of Semitic origin, that is, the descendants of Shem, one of the sons of Noah. The word "Hebrew" goes back to Noah's great-great-great-grandson, Heber. According to Jewish tradition, Eber refused to participate in the construction of the Tower of Babel, preserving the Hebrew language. Later the Hebrews were known as Jews, a word originating in Judah, one of the tribes of Israel.

So the sovereignty of God was centered on the Hebrews, the places where they were: in the wilderness, in Egypt, in Israel and the peoples who were related to the Hebrews: the Egyptians, the Edomites, the Philistines, etc.

God's interest was centered on his chosen people and it was in this limited universe that God especially used his sovereignty after creation.

God, for example, did not intervene militarily or in the history of indigenous American nations, which did not feel the hand of God's sovereignty. Likewise, it did not intervene in this way in the millennial nation of China and so on.

The sovereignty of God has another characteristic: that of being episodic.

In the approximately 10,000 years of history reported by the Bible, the events in which

God intervened actively in the human will are told in one hand.

The favorite example of the adherents of divine determinism is the episode of the hardening of Pharaoh's heart.

First, Pharaoh was already stubbornly decided. God simply intensified that feeling. The main reasons for the hardening were not so that the glory and majesty of God would be manifested, but rather to allow a sustainable exodus of the people, because Pharaoh had the secret B plan to free the Hebrews to killlos on the way out of Egypt by way of the Egyptian escort that would accompany them and also because, even if there was liberation at that time, the Hebrews would leave Egypt with nothing: few food and no goods. This was not written in the Bible for a simple reason: God is sovereign and gives no explanation to man. For this reason, the Bible gives no greater explanation of God's motives for the use of his sovereignty, which serves his good and lofty purposes. But all decisions have had and have God's reasons and the choice rests on the best alternative.

Still in relation to this episode, God did not suppress Pharaoh's will completely. God contributed to this will bending towards what Pharaoh had already decided in his heart.

How often has God hardened the human heart? Throughout the Bible this is the one and only account.

The Bible does indeed report an example of almost suppression of the human will. It's the Prophet Jonah episode. The Prophet Jonah had practically no freedom to flee from God. He spent three days inside the big fish. This interference was episodic and therefore discontinued. But we can say that the negative decision resulted from his fragile psychic condition, given that he was hermaphrodite and was depressed, and God healed him and he became an important prophet.

We have already talked about when God intervened in the human will in the above two examples. God can also interfere with facts and events.

This intervention in events is common in biblical accounts. It is when God acts in History and in the facts performing His will without interfering decisively in human will. God opened the Red Sea for the passage of the Hebrews. It brings water out of the rock. God chooses people for certain missions and deposes them, choosing kings and queens, missionaries, pastors and priests.

God sovereignly uses his power for his good purposes. As expressed in Psalm 33:6-11:

> "By the word of the Lord were the heavens made, and the heavenly bodies by the breath of his mouth.
>
> He gathers the waters of the sea in one place, from the depths he makes reservoirs.

> Let all the earth fear the Lord; Let all the inhabitants of the world tremble before him.
>
> For he spake, and it was done; He ordered it, and it all came out.
>
> The Lord undoes the plans of the nations and frustrates the purposes of the peoples.
>
> But the Lord's plans remain forever, the purposes of his heart, for all generations."

But God does not always act alone in the accomplishment of his good purposes. Very commonly he acts synergistically in partnership with Man.

God sovereignly chooses people for certain missions, but in the next moment these people have a good margin of discretion to accept the mission or not. God did not compel Moses to accept the mission of leading the Hebrews out of Egypt, although he insisted heavily on this point. God spoke to Moses and was understanding when Moses argued that he could not speak in public. God then appointed Moses' brother, Aaron, for this specific task.

When God intervenes through association with Man he acts in a generally particularized way with people who will lead his people. Thus God chose in Israel kings, judges, and priests for the purpose of leading, defending, instructing, and disciplining His chosen people.

God chose kings and priests, but they must accept the mission on the basis of the responsible will of which they were endowed.

Therefore, God's intervention in human history has always been punctual, episodic, localized, particularized and exceptional.

But why does God not appear among clouds on the noble TV channel and proclaim his majesty to the whole world to hear. Or why does he not intervene in all acts and facts so that all may believe and serve him?

This is due to two main reasons: 1) God granted free will to the Human Being, that is, the ability to make choices for himself. Where there is free will there is no divine sovereignty; 2) God chose faith as one of the criteria of salvation, being incompatible with the sovereignty of God, that is, if everything were under the sovereignty of God, faith would be completely unnecessary, because all things would be seen and perceived.

Another important aspect is that many divine manifestations cannot be considered as externalization of divine sovereignty, because, more often than not, God acts in association with human will; At other times the power of God is released in fulfillment of a promise without there being a specific, actual, and completely free decision from God.

We have seen that sovereignty means control resulting from an exclusive, unconditional, concrete, specific and current decision.

We can then exclude from the concept of sovereignty the acts of partnership with the Human Being and the acts in which divine power is released in fulfillment of a promise. These acts are conditioned.

In the first case, we have the occurrence of a synergy with the competing will and efforts of God and man. If any of these actors does not collaborate, there is no performance of the act.

If God chooses and the person does not accept, the synergy is not realized and God will use plan B to achieve his goals.

For example, in the raising up of kings and prophets, God chooses sovereignly, but the cycle is only completed with the acceptance of the mission, and for this there is an act of partnership of God with Man, from which a synergy is born, that is, a collaboration of efforts and will toward the purposes of the Kingdom of God.

Nor will there be sovereignty when the act is carried out in fulfillment of a promise without a concrete, specific and actual decision of God.

Better to explain, all God's actions derive from his decisions. But there are decisions taken beforehand and hypothetically by God that will only be completed in the future if they satisfy the conditions laid down. When these conditions are met concretely in the future, the power of God is released without there being a new, case-specific decision of God.

This occurs in relation to some miracles and the descent commonly performed by the Holy Spirit. In these two cases, the invariable condition is faith and also repentance for the second example.

If the Holy Spirit were to determine all the actions of the called and the chosen, from repentance to conversion, we should logically conclude that this is the work of God's sovereignty and, as such, an exclusive action of God.

However, the action of the Holy Spirit is associated with human will, there being a synergy, a union of efforts, will, and action on the part of both God and man.

And the Holy Spirit does not have the function of determining the meaning of people's will, but rather of distributing spiritual gifts, consoling, convincing humanity of sin, of judgment, and that Jesus is the Savior.

We must also bear in mind that the Holy Spirit comes only to him who is prepared to receive His presence. The Holy Spirit does not violate human will. He is a gentleman.

Returning to the tension between will and sovereignty, the reader of the Bible notes that there are not only many Bible verses speaking of our freedom, but there are also many verses dealing with God's interference in human will and situations.

On the one hand, the Bible says, "Knock, and it shall be opened unto you" (Mt 7:7), "come unto me them that labour and are heavy laden" (Mt 11:28), "I would gather them together as a hen gathers her young chicks, but ye would not" (Mt 23:37) and "that whosoever believeth in her shall have eternal life." (John 3:16).

The parables of the Nazarene also accentuate the will and human collaboration in the Kingdom of God, like the parable of the sower, in which the seed is sown in different soils that represent the human heart: fertile, stony, thorny. The parable of the talents also emphasizes human participation, praising the one who reproduced the talents and censoring what he buried in the ground. The parable of the widow and the wicked judge. The parable of the lamp.

On the other hand, the Bible says, "He only comes to me who my Father brings me" (Jn 6:37), "no sparrow falls from heaven unless the Father allows it" (Mt 10:29), "from the beginning God chose them to be saved" (2 Thess 2:13)", "no hair falls from their heads unless God allows it" (Lk 21:18).

But, logically, there can be no sovereignty where there is a responsible will, and therefore the problem of this coexistence is considered an antinomy, that is, two antagonistic truths that coexist in the Bible.

This tension of diametrically opposed forces caused some to defend the coexistence of these two actions. There would be the responsible-will, that is, the human power to make choices and, at the same time, the divine power to interfere completely in human will and situations. This, however, is logically incompatible, as we have already seen in previous lines.

Let's look at some verses. The verses of the sparrow and the hair do not refer to God's intervention on the human will, they refer to the possible intervention in facts and situation. Thus, here we have no antinomy, because the will-responsible is preserved. Furthermore, it is important to note that the verse is addressed to the Apostles, not to every Christian.

As to Jesus' assertion that only the Father will bring to him, this means the diversity of functions of the Heavenly Council. Jehovah is the Holy Spirit in identifying the person who, hearing the Word, repents and is led to Jesus to dwell in it.

As for the elect for salvation, chosen from the beginning of the world, they are the ones who, among many, will receive the special divine call. Every call of God has as its ultimate purpose the salvation of the one who has received the call. This, however, does not mean that the call, or even the chosen one, is previously saved, or that it will endure to the end.

The Heavenly Council assures that no one will be saved a priori, that is, no one will be saved without an evaluation. Even the one to whom God does not blame should have his merit.

God can elect people at any time and this election means that they will be called to serve the Kingdom of Heaven. Whether the called will accept the invitation, or, after accepting it, whether they will persevere to the end, is another matter.

In conclusion, I would like to mention a few important points on the subject:

1º) It is important to distinguish the interference of God now at work in the human will and now at work in the events. In events, there will always be sovereignty of God except if divine power is conditional, released in fulfillment of a promise. In the case of interference in the human will, there will never be sovereignty of God properly so called, but rather a partnership between God and man, entering both the will and efforts for the accomplishment of God's good purposes;

2º) The sovereignty of God is located in places, peoples and persons according to divine purposes, and God acts through chosen persons who freely accept the mission;

3º) The sovereignty of God is episodic, arising as an exception;

4º) The exceptionality of divine sovereignty stems from having chosen God the faith as one of the criteria of relationship with the Human Being and salvation.

These are the notes I made. Of course, the subject would deserve much more study, but I hope that these guidelines can illuminate the interpretation of the Bible.

8.   Free Will in the Vision of Calvinism and Arminianism

One cannot speak of free will or, as I prefer to say, of responsible will, not to mention Calvinism and Arminianism.

They take care of two different theological systems.

Jacobus Arminius, Latinized name of Jakob Hermanszoon, born on 10 October 1560 and died on 19.10.1609, was a Dutch pastor and theologian (from the Netherlands, present-day Holland), and professor of theology at the University of Leiden, writer of many books and treatises on theology.

John Calvin was a French theologian, writer and religious leader, who lived from 10/07/1509 to 27/05/1564, preceding Arminius in a generation and recognized as one of the leading leaders of the consolidation of the Protestant Reformation initiated by Martin Luther who posted his 95 theses at the door of Wittenberg Cathedral on 31/10/1517.

Arminius opposed the ideas of John Calvin, which were later systematized into what would be called Calvinism.

According to the widipédia, in the title "Aminianism", Arminian theology "did not become fully developed during Arminius' lifetime; only after his death (1609) did the five articles of remonstrance (1610) systematize and formalize his ideas".

Indeed, about one year after the death of Jacobus Arminius, 45 ministers who were his followers signed and presented to the Dutch State a theological declaration called Remonstrance (1610), which means "admonition" or "protest" in English, which gathered 5 articles of faith, that postulated changes in the Belgian Confession, Heidelberg

Catechism and doctrines of the Dutch Church, containing the following 5 points:

1. depravity is total, but there is free will from the receiving of grace. Arminius declared: "In this state (fallen), man's free will for the true good is not only wounded, ill, inclined and weakened; but he is also trapped, destroyed and lost. And his powers are not only weakened and useless unless assisted by grace, but have no power except when animated by divine grace". Justification and also condemnation depend on the rational faith, or non-faith of man;

2. The atonement, though qualitatively sufficient to all men, is only effective to the man of faith;

3. justification is possible for all, but only reaches those who have faith in Jesus. Without the aid of the Holy Spirit, no person is able to respond to the will of God;

4. grace is resistible; and

5. believers are able to resist sin, but are not out of the possibility of falling from grace.

In the period 13/11/1618 to 09/05/1619, was formed the International Synod of Dordt, or of Dordt or Dordrecht, convened by the States General by the Dutch Reformed Church and held in Dordrecht, in the Netherlands, which aimed to regulate the controversy series installed in the Dutch Churches since the rise of Arminianism, having counted on the participation of guests coming from 8 foreign countries with voting rights.

The synod rejected Arminian ideas, establishing the Reformed doctrine on five points: total depravity, unconditional election, limited atonement, effective calling (or irresistible grace) and perseverance of the saints. These doctrines contained in the final document called "Canons of Dort", are also known as the "Five Points of Calvinism".

In total opposition to the points of Arminianism, except partial agreement on the first point, are the 5 points of Calvinism, which proposes the following:

1st- man, from his birth, is totally depraved, slave to sin and naturally rebellious to God, unable to please or obey God and not being able to accomplish what is truly good in the eyes of God, nor to prepare for salvation. There is no free will, even for regenerated man.

God sovereignly chooses to whom he will grant the grace of salvation. According to the Wikipédia, in the title Five Points of Calvinism, "this choice is not based on any moral or individual merit, or even on the faith of the people whom He chooses; but rather in its sovereign, unconditional, irrevocable and unfathomable decision, "conferring upon the elect faith and grace.

3rd- only the elect - and all of them, are justified to salvation, complete in the death of Christ. The work of Jesus aimed at the salvation of those who were previously chosen by God. The saving efficacy of Christ would not be "universal" or "potentially effective" for those who would receive it, but specifically designed to consolidate the salvation of the chosen before the foundation of the world.

4th- grace reaches the elect and it comes irresistibly, so that every elect has grace and is converted, and everyone who has grace is an elect. Conversion is the exclusive action of God and the Holy Spirit, being irresistible to man.

5th - all the elect - and only these, will necessarily persevere to the end, that is, they will not decay from grace or lose salvation.

The five points of Calvinism are known by the acrostic "TULIP", referring to the initials of the points in English, as follows:

In English	Free translation
T - Total Depravity	Total Depravity
U - Unconditional Election	Unconditional Election
L - Limited Atonement	Limited Atonement
I - Irresistible Grace	Graça Irresistible
P - Perseverance of the Saints	Perseverance of the Saints

It is very illuminating the picture published in the Wikipédia under the title "Arminianism", which makes a comparison between the Arminian points in relation to Lutheranism and Calvinism, as it reads in the following page:

THEME	LUTHERANISM	CALVINISM	ARMINIANISM
HUMAN WILL	Total depravity without free will	Total depravity without free will	Total depravity, with free will from grace
ELECTION	Unconditional, only election for salvation	Unconditional election to salvation.	Conditional election, based on faith or foreseen unbelief
JUSTIFICATION	Justification of all who believe completely in the death of Christ	Justification is limited to the elect to salvation, complete in the death of Christ	Justification is possible for all, but only applies to those who put faith in Jesus
CONVERSION	Monergista through the means of grace, resistable	Monergist, without means, irresistible	Synergist, free will restored by prevenient grace, able to resist the gospel, but without human merit if he receives the gift of faith.
PRESERVATION AND APOSTASY	Falling from grace is possible, but God gives assurance of preservation	Perseverance of the saints: the eternally elect in Christ will necessarily persevere in faith and holiness to the end	Preservation is conditioned to continued faith in Christ; there is possibility of a total and definitive apostasy

In summary, soteriology (part of the theology that deals with the salvation of man), defended by Calvinism, has as "axis the statement that God is perfectly capable of saving every person He intends to make object of His saving grace and that His work cannot be thwarted by something or someone who gets in the way in an attempt to prevent its completion" (Wikipédia, "Five Points of Calvinism").

On the other hand, Arminianism argues that the free will of the human person accompanies the process of conversion, justification and salvation, constituting an element of affirmation of his dignity.

We then have the adherents of Monergism (Calvinists) and the adherents of Synergy (Arminians). While the former hold that salvation originates wholly from God, the latter claim that although the whole of salvation proceeds solely from God, the process of receiving salvation involves the voluntary faith of man who receives empowering grace.

It is important to stand before these two soteriological views. Not that they interfere with your salvation: you will be saved, or not, according to biblical criteria and not according to the acceptance of one or another doctrine.

9. Weaknesses of Calvinism and Arminianism

Both the Points of Calvinism and the Points of Arminianism did not come out of the pure inventiveness of their advocates.

These points resulted from accurate analyses and interpretations of the Holy Scriptures by serious scholars who point either one way or the other.

However, as the starting point of the proposition of the points has always been the Scriptures, the isolated and literal interpretation has often led to illogical and disconnected conclusions from reality.

Let us then, point by point, look first at the two systems and then at the Five Points of each of the schools

9.1 The Fragility of Systems

In the foreground, the two soteriological systems do not comprise all the hypotheses of salvation, constituting incomplete systems.

They are systems because the five points of each school are the result of a logical sequence: while Calvinism starts from the premise that there is no free will, and man is found to be a slave to his sins, Rminianism has as its premise the possibility that man can have faith.

However, they are closed and incomplete systems, because they deal exclusively with salvation through Jesus Christ.

Jesus is the only way to salvation for those who will not go to trial and who have been regenerated, persevering to the end, as Jesus of Nazareth assured:

> Verily, verily, I say unto you, He that heareth my word, and believeth on him that sent me, hath not eternal life, but is passed from death unto life (John 5:24, BO, Jesus of Nazareth).

However, there will be billions of people who do not believe in Jesus as their savior and many others who may even believe in Jesus, but have not been regenerated and do not follow the teachings of Christ. Many others do not even believe in God, or believe in other gods.

These people will not be simply and aprioristically cast into hell as some think.

All these people, who are without Jesus, will be judged at the Great Heavenly Tribunal, where they can be redeemed, or not, according to a simple criterion: the practice of justice, of giving to each one what is due according to the conscience that God has endowed all human beings.

In other words, in principle, the criterion will be to verify whether these people loved their fellow man as themselves.

But one might argue, "But this is unjust: I believed and followed Jesus all my life".

No, it would be unfair to condemn all unregenerate people without trial.

Moreover, the righteousness of God will also be verified in the assignment of reward after the heavenly admission, which will form the hierarchy and discipline among heavenly beings.

It is certain that the martyrs for Christ will receive a great reward and those regenerated in Christ a special reward, provided that both have kept the Scriptures, while those who will be saved without Jesus will receive a substantially lesser reward.

The two systems we are studying propose that there is no free will, nor salvation, without regeneration by the Holy Spirit.

For a statement to be logically true, it must be valid for all hypotheses.

Thus, if, among trillions of people, one finds himself only a person who is just and qualified for salvation, although he does not have Jesus, it is concluded that the soteriological systems studied are incomplete, fragile and false.

Because they are limited and incomplete systems, both Arminian and Calvinist points cannot express affirmative or negative propositions regarding unelected persons (Calvinistic system) or people without faith in Jesus (Arminian system).

This is perfectly understood when one considers that such soteriological systems are closed and specific to certain people.

These systems cannot conclude, for example, that only the elect (Calvinism) will be saved, or only for those who have faith (Arminianism), since the righteous, even without regeneration, can also be reached by salvation.

These systems can, at most, propose that salvation occurs for the elect and for those who have faith in Jesus, without being able to amplify the assertion to deny salvation to people not understood in these closed systems.

Same reasoning applies to the third point (justification): systems cannot claim that people - not understood in the system, are considered as "not justified".

9.2   Point one: Depravity

At this point, both systems agree that there would be total depravity of the human being, proposing Calvinism that this condition endures even after regeneration, specific point on which the Arminianism disagrees that admits human ability to choose freely after regeneration.

The picture painted by these Systems is that people are blindfolded and have earplugs, walking directly into the abyss whose fall is fatal.

While Arminianism proposes that God goes after this population, crying, "Return, repent, see the death of my only begotten Son; take off the tampons and the mask and see"; Calvinism proposes that God tears off the masks and tampons of those He has chosen and they have a vivifying uproar before falling into the precipice.

Of course, this is a painting painted by the Calvinists.

However, we have already studied that it is illogical to say that the human being does not have free will.

It may be a diminished free will by the necessary and occasional antecedents, but there will always be a substantial margin of a constant free will.

To say that the human being has no freedom of action is to distance himself from reality.

People make substantially free decisions all the time regardless of whether they are Christian or not.

Many decisions are good, even if the author is not a Christian. Atheists can also do good deeds.

Gandhi exclaimed at a certain opportunity that he admired Christianity, but disliked Christians, emphasizing the distance between speech and practice.

Jesus Christ taught that He did not come to save the righteous, but sinners. The sane don't need a doctor, just the sick.

Can it be harder to find righteous people among the unregenerate?

This is true, because regeneration is a powerful antecedent to the human psyche, but we can find a considerable number of righteous people among the unregenerate, who truly love their neighbor and practice good deeds most of the time.

Jesus of Nazareth taught that evil people also give good things to their children in the likeness of good parents (Mt 7:9-11), showing that goodness is a human choice.

If we had to choose a school to adhere to on the question of free will, we would join Sepfollowed Pelagianism, in the sense that the human being receives strong influence from the Adamic inheritance (tendency to sin), but this does not affect it to the point of preventingto make free choices.

Many biblical passages proclaim the freedom of the person to act, such as: Luke 7:30, in which Jesus of Nazareth states that the Pharisees and the interpreters of the law rejected the plan of God, presumably offered to them in the same way as to all others; John 7:17, in which the Nazarene presupposes the existence of Jews who want to do the will of God, which enables them to know the doctrine that He preached; 1 Cor 7:37, in which Paul of Tarsus praises those who have dominion over their own will, and admonishes them to remain unmarried; 1º Cor 10:13, in which Paul of Tarsus states that temptations can be overcome with the forces of the Christian.

Also in the Old Testament, we find biblical passages that highlight the free choices of the people, such as: Exodus 35:29; 36:3; Deut 12:6 and 17 and Deut 16:10, Lev 7:16; 22:18, 21 and 23; Lev 23:381, 2nd Chr 31:14 and 35:8; Amos 4:5, Ezra 1:4 and 6, 3:5, 7:16 and 8:28; Num 15:3 and 29:39; where the people brought voluntary offerings to the Lord; Isaiah 1:19-20, in which God offers the choice between listening to him and rejecting him; Psalms 119:10

and 108, in which the Psalmist exclaims that he sought God and offered offerings with his lips.

The emblematic passage of human freedom in the Old Testament is found in Deuteronomy 30:19, which reads:

> The heavens and the earth have I this day borne witness against thee, that I have set before thee life and death, blessing and curse: Choose therefore the life, that thou mayest live, thou, and thy seed (Jehovah, BO).

It is also important to highlight that, for soteriology, what should be considered is the use of freedom and not exactly free will.

On previous lines, we have distinguished between the power of the will and the power of the act.

While the power of the will is tied to free will, the power of the act is related to the freedom to act.

I can want one thing and accomplish another, or I can want something and practice the desired act.

They do not always coincide with wanting and achieving it.

For Jesus, the most important measure of salvation is the power of acting, that is, how you use your freedom.

Jesus told the parable of the two sons, according to which the father asks one of his sons to go to work in the vineyard, and he initially refused to go, but repented and went to work in the vineyard. The father reached the second son and made the same request. The second son said "I am coming," but he did not go (Mt 21:28-30).

Through this parable, Jesus taught that the father's will was only heeded by the first son, who did what he asked, although he said initially that he would not do it.

It may be that God elects thoughts as a criterion for granting only the reward.

Among the verses cited by the defenders of Calvinism for the conclusion of total depravity are Gen 6:5 and Rom 3:10-18.

The first verse speaks of people in Noah's time, and the second verse says that the heart is deceptive, i.e., that the first sentimental reaction can be deceptive. But this reaction is subjected to a mental assessment and value judgment, not meaning that the first reaction prevails and defines the person's conduct. The deceitful heart equates with the malicious inclination of the human being.

In relation to Romans 3, the predicate "there is none righteous, not one" (Rom 3:10) refers to the subject "the foolish" of Psalm 14:1.

The existence of the righteous is documented throughout the Bible, and Jesus said that He did not come to save the righteous.

I have selected some important passages for understanding the theme:

> For he that will love life, and see happy days, restrain the tongue of evil, and prevent his lips from speaking deceitfully;
>
> Turn away from evil, do what is good, seek peace, and strive to achieve it.
>
> For the eyes of the Lord rest upon the righteous, and his ears are open unto their supplications: but the face of the Lord is against them that do evil. (1 Peter 3:8-12, quoting Psalm 34:12-16)

But a man shall say, You have faith, and I have works; Shew me thy faith without works, and I will shew thee my faith with works.

You see that a person is justified by works and not by faith alone.

Likewise was not the harlot Rahab also justified by works, when she received the messengers, and sent them out another way?

For as the body without spirit is dead, so faith without works is dead also. (James 2:18 and 24-26)

Blessed are the humble in spirit, for theirs is the kingdom of heaven.

Blessed are they that mourn, for they shall be comforted.

Blessed are the merciful, for they shall obtain mercy.

Blessed are the pure in heart, for they shall see God.

(Bo, Jesus, Matthew 5:3,4,7 and 8).

And it came to pass, as he sat at meat in the house, many publicans and sinners came and took their places with Jesus and his disciples.

And when the Pharisees saw it, they said unto his disciples, Why eateth your Master with publicans and sinners? But when Jesus heard it, he said, The sane need not a physician, but the sick.

But go and learn what it means:

I want mercy, not burnt offerings; for I am not come to call the righteous, but sinners (to repentance).

(Matthew 9:10-13, BO, Jesus Christ)

And into whatever city or town you enter, inquire who in them is worthy; and stay there until you retire.

When you enter the house, hear it;

If the house be worthy, let your peace come upon it: But if it be not so, let your peace be unto you" (Matthew 10:11-13, Jesus Christ, BO).

It is also argued that there are at least three persons declared to be righteous by the Holy Scriptures in the New Testament, which are: Zechariah and Elizabeth, parents of John the Baptist, according to Luke 1:5 and 6, and Simeon, considered righteous and godly according to Luke 2:25.

Then the experience of life and observation show that there are a number of people who are righteous even if they are not religious, or who profess a religion distinct from Christianity.

There is, therefore, no exclusivity of salvation for Christians, but exclusivity of the regenerated to reach the heavens without judgment.

9.3   2nd Point: Election

The systems in question start from the mistaken premise that election is a selection of God so that some people, and only these, come to salvation.

For them, God would have selected some people at the foundation of the world to be saved. Only such persons would be saved; the rest would be thrown into the fires of hell regardless of what they have done, even because both Calvinism and Rminianism believe in the total corruption of the human being.

Without divine help, no person can be saved according to the premise adopted by these systems, because all people are dead in their sins.

But election is not, and never has been, a prioristic judgment of God.

The elect are not to salvation; They were chosen to receive a special call from the Holy Spirit. God's purpose is that all people be saved, and for so many, all people are called ordinarily, but only the elect receive an extraordinary or special call.

The election is not positioned within the soteriology, at least not directly.

The Apostle Peter states that the elect are for obedience to God as 1 Peter 1:1.

It is also important to stress that the non-elect can be saved and many have achieved this victory and that many elect will not be saved.

I would like to quote some biblical passages to help in understanding the theme:

> Come unto me, all ye that labour and are heavy laden, and I will give you rest (Mt 11:28, Jesus Christ, BO).

> First of all, therefore, I exhort you to use the practice of supplications, prayers,

intercessions, thanksgiving, on behalf of all men...

This is good and acceptable before God, our Savior, who desires all men to be saved and to come to the knowledge of the truth (1 Timothy 2:1-4).

For God so loved the world that he gave his only begotten Son, that whosoever believeth in him should not perish, but have eternal life (John 3:16, Jesus of Nazareth, BO).

Now if ye call upon him as the Father, who without respect of persons judgeth according to the works of every man, behave yourselves with fear during the time of your sojourning (1 Peter 1:17).

Judges and officers shalt thou make thee in all thy cities, which the LORD thy God giveth thee among thy tribes, to judge the people with right judgment.

Thou shalt not wrest righteousness, thou shalt not respect persons... (Deut 16:18-19, Jehovah, BUS).

Peter, an apostle of Jesus Christ, to the elect who are strangers of the dispersion in Pontus, Galatia, Cappadocia, Asia, and Bithynia, chosen according to the foreknowledge of God the Father, in sanctification of the Spirit, for obedience and sprinkling of the blood of Jesus Christ, Grace to you and peace be multiplied (1st Pet 1:1, Apostle Peter, BO).

Also, in this same direction, the following Biblical verses: John 4:42, Rom 9:30, Rom 5:1-2, Eph 1:13, 1 Tim 4:10.

9.4 3rd Point: Atonement

Considering the premises previously made, the regenerates and the righteous will be justified, regardless of whether they have been elected, or not, and the cross of Jesus will reach the regenerates who persevere to the end and the others will be submitted to judgment by justice.

The cross of Jesus has enough power to potentially save all people, but the regenerated will be saved who persevere to the end and the righteous who, while not believing in the divine sonship of Jesus, actually obey His teachings.

I quote some passages to help you understand the theme:

For God so loved the world that He gave His only begotten Son, that whosoever believeth in Him should not perish, but have everlasting life (BO, Disciple John, John 3:16).

Indeed, the will of my Father is that every man who sees the Son and believes in him should have eternal life; and I will raise him up at the last day (Mt 6:40, BO, Jesus of Nazareth).

I am the living bread which came down from heaven; If any man eat thereof, he shall live for ever: And the bread that I will give for the life of the world is my flesh (John 6:51, Jesus of Nazareth, BO).

Tribulation and distress shall come upon the soul of any man that doeth evil, to the Jew first, and also to the Greek:

But glory, and honour, and peace, to every one that doeth good, to the first Jew, and also to the Greek.

For there is no partiality with God.

For as many as have sinned without law shall perish without law: And all they that have sinned by law shall be judged.

For the simple hearers of the law are not righteous before God: but they that do the law shall be justified.

For when the Gentiles, which have no law, do by nature according to the law, having no law, they serve the law for themselves.

These show the standard of the law engraved in their hearts, also witnessing to their conscience and their thoughts, mutually accusing or defending themselves, in the day when God, through Christ Jesus, judges the secrets of men, in accordance with my gospel (Paul of Tarsus, BO, Rom 2:9-16).

And through him (Jesus of Nazareth) every one that believeth is justified of all things of which ye could not be justified by the law of Moses (Acts 13:39, Luke, BUS).

In this sense, the following biblical portions: Is 53:6, Mt 11:28-30, Mt 18:14, Jn 1:7, Heb 2:9, Heb 10:10, 2nd Pe 3:9, 1st Jn 4:14 and 2:2, Jn 4:42, Re 22:17, Jn 1:29, Jn 3:16-17, 6:33 and 51, 12:47, Rom 3:23-24, Rom 5:6, Rm 5:15, Rom 10:13, 2 Co 5:14-15, 1 Tim 4:10 and 2:3-6, Titus 2:11.

9.5   4th Point: Grace

Conversion is available to all people, since the Holy Spirit acts upon all people who can repent of their sins, even with the help of the Holy Spirit.

But not all are regenerated, because they have not placed themselves in the service of God completely.

Therefore, grace can be resisted by the person in the use of his freedom, even if it has been elected from the foundation of the world.

For a better understanding, I quote a few verses related to the possibility of resisting grace:

> Wherefore, brethren, seek more and more diligently to confirm your calling and election; For in so doing ye shall not stumble at any time.
>
> For in this way you will be amply supplied with the entrance into the eternal kingdom of our Lord and Savior Jesus Christ (2 Peter 1:10-11).

Also in this sense we find the following passages: Lk 7:30, Acts 7:51, Rom 10:16, 2nd Cor 6:1, Rom 11:17-24, 1st Cor 15:2, Eph 5:3-7, Col 1:21 A 23, 2nd Pe 2:20-22, Heb 6:4-6, Heb 10:26, Jas 1:12 and 5:19-20.

9.6   5th Point: Preservation of the Saints

The saints or regenerates can fall from grace, giving up salvation and making use of their freedom.

Thus, the passage must be understood with the dialogue of Jesus Christ: "I give unto them eternal life; They shall never perish, neither shall any man pluck them out of my hand" (John 10:28; BO; Jesus Christ), because no external force can separate us from Christ, unless the person himself departs by his liberality.

I quote some verses in favor of my conclusion:

> You shall be hated of all men for my name's sake; But he that endureth to the end, the same shall be saved (Mk 13:13; Jesus Christ; BO).

> But he that endureth to the end, the same shall be saved (Mt 24:13; Jesus Christ; BO).

> Therefore, if, after they have escaped the defilements of the world through the knowledge of the Lord and Saviour Jesus Christ, they become entangled again and are overcome, their last state has become worse than the first.

> For it had been better for them never to have known the way of righteousness than, having known it, to turn back from the holy

commandment given to them (2 Pet 2:20-21, Apostle Peter, BO).

10. Bibliographic References

1. *The Living Bible.* Several translators. 10. ed. São Paulo: Editora Mundo Cristão, 1997.

2. *The Jerusalem Bible.* Several translators. São Paulo: Pauline Editions, 1981.

3. *The New Life Bible.* Translated by João Ferreira de Almeida. 2. ed. São Paulo: S. R. Edições Vida Nova, 1978.

4. AQUINO, Thomas. *The Free Will (Questiones Disputatae de Veritate - Question 24)".* Translation, edition and notes: Paulo Faltanin and Bernardo Veiga. São Paulo: EDIPRO, 2015.

5. AUGUSTIN, Aurelius (Saint Augustine; Bishop of Hippo). "Grace and free will". Translated from the English original "A Treatise on Grace and Free Will". Amazon.

6. BAHNSEN, Greg L. and others. *Law and Gospel: Five Points of View".* Translation Valdemar Kroker. São

Paulo: Editora Vida, 2003.

7. *Bible of New International Studies.* Editora Vida, 2003.

8. *Bible of the Worker.* Translated by João Ferreira de Almeida. Revised and updated. 2nd ed. Barueri - SP: Brazilian Biblical Society, 2007.

9. *Complete Jewish Bible: the Tanakk (OT) and the B'Rit Hadashah (NT).* Translation of the original into English by David H. Stern; Portuguese translation Rogério Portella, Celso Eronides Fernandes - São Paulo: Editora Vida, 2010.

10. *Ecumenical Bible Translation. Editions Loyola, 1994.*

11. BERKOUWER, G.C. *Biblical* Doctrine of Sin. São Paulo: Editora Aste, 1970.

12. BLOOM, Paul. *What makes us good or bad.* Translated by Eduardo Rieche. Best Seller, 2014. Title in English: "Just Babies". E-book available on Amazon.

13. BRUCE, MICHAEL and another (STEVEN BARBONE). *The 100 Most Important Arguments of Western Philosophy.* São Paulo: Editora Cultrix, 2013.

14. CARSON, Donald A. The *Gagged God: Christianity*

confronts pluralism. Translation of Lena Spider and Regina Spider. São Paulo: Shedd Publications, 2013.

15. CHADWICK, Henry and G. R. Evans. *"Christian Church".* Translated by Carlos Nougué and Francisco Manhães. Barcelona: Ediciones Folio S.A., 2004.

16. COENEN, Lothar and others (COLIN BROWN). *"International* Dictionary of New Testament Theology".* 2 volumes; 2nd ed. São Paulo: Religious Society New Life Editions, 2000.

17. DANTAS. *"Civil Law Program".* 4th ed. 4th edition Editora Rio.

18. Portuguese Dictionary - Hebrew / Hebrew - Portuguese. Abraham Hatzamri and Shoshana More-Hatzamri. Editora e Livraria Sêfer Ltda, 2000.

19. DREHER, A. *Martin Luther, the Interpreter of the Gospel.* São Leopoldo: Synodal Publishing.

20. EARLE, E. Cairns. *Christianity through the Ages. A History of the Christian Church. Translation Israel Belo de Azevedo, Valdemar Kroker.* 3rd ed. São Paulo: Vida Nova, 2008.

21. EHRMAN, Bart D. *Problem with God.* Translated by Alexandre Martins. Rio de Janeiro: Agir, 2008.

22. FERREIRA, Franklin. *The Christian Church in History.* From the origins to the present day. São Paulo: New Life, 2013.

23. FLUSSER. *Jesus. Editora Perspectiva, 2002.*

24. GILL, John. *Considerations about the love of God.* Amazon e-book.

25. Great Encyclopedia Larousse Cultural. Nova Cultural, 1998.

26. GRUDEM, Wayne. Systematic Theology current and exhaustive. Translation Norio Yamakami, Lucy Yamakami, Luiz A. T. Sayão, Eduardo Pereira e Ferreira. São Paulo: New Life, 1999.

27. Gundry. Law and Gospel. Publisher Vida. 1996. Collection Theological debates.

28. HUCKABEE, Davis W. Based on grace: studies in central doctrines of the Christian faith. E-book published by Amazon. Edited by Ministry Word Pending. São José dos Campos (SP), 2016.

29. KRUGER, C. Baxter. Cabana. Rio de Janeiro: Sextante.

30. KRUGER, C. Baxter. *Back to the Cabin.* Translated by André Costa and Sônia Schwarts. Rio de Janeiro: Sextante, 2011.

31. Kruse, Walter. *Seeking Communion with the Living God.* Editora Oxigênio, 2011.

32. Kruse, Walter. *The (in)conditional love of God: first part.* Author's edition. Amazon e-book, 2016.

33. Kruse, Walter. The (in)conditional love of God: second part. Author's edition. Amazon e-book, 2016; printed version through the Authors Club.

34. LACOSTE, Jean-Yves. *Critical* Dictionary of Theology. Translation Paulo Meneses. São Paulo: Paulinas: Edições Loyola, 2004.

35. LANGE, Nicholas. *Jewish* People. Translated by Carlos Nougué, Francisco Manães, Maria Julia Braga, Joana Bergman. Barcelona. Ediciones Folio S.A., 2007.

36. LAW, Stephen. *Zahar Illustrated* Guide: Philosophy. Translation Maria Luíza X. de A. Borges; Danilo Marcondes. 3rd ed. Rio de Janeiro: Zahar Editora,

2011.

37. LAWRENCE, Paul. *Historical and Geographical* Atlas of the Bible. Translated by Suzana Klassen and Vanderlei Orgigoza. Barueri-SP: Biblical Society of Brazil, 2008.

38. LEWIS, C. S. "The *Problem of Suffering*".

39. LUTHER, Martin. *The Freedom of the Christian.* Editora Escala.

40. M'Cheyne, Robert Murray. *A believer takes pleasure in the law of God.* Amazon e-book.

41. MIEN, Aleksandr. *Jesus Master of Nazareth. New Town Publishing House, 2002.*

42. MORIN, Emile. *Jesus and the Structures of His Time".* *São Paulo: Pauline Editions, 1981.*

43. NEE, Watchman. *The Normal Christian Life.* São Paulo: Editora Fiel Ltda., 1979.

44. New Testament Greek English. Translation by Vilson Scholz; includes the text of the translation of João Ferreira de Almeida. Barueri-SP: Biblical Society of Brazil, 2008.

45. OLSON, Roger. *History of Controversies in Christian Theology*. São Paulo: Editora Vida, 2004.

46. OWEN, John. *Against Arminianism and its Pelagian idol, free will.* Amazon e-book.

47. *"The Foundations: The Famous Collection of Texts of Fundamental Biblical Truths.* Edited by R.A. Torrey and updated L. Frinberg and others. Several writers. São Paulo: Editora Hagnos, 2005.

48. OWEN, John. Against Aminianism and its Pelagian idol", free will. Amazon e-book.

49. PERKS. Stephen C. *Worship of Baal: ancient and modern. Amazon e-book.*

50. PETERSON, Eugene H. The Message: *The Bible in Contemporary Language.* Exegetical and theological supervision Luiz Sayão. São Paulo: Editora Vida, 2011.

51. PLANTINGA. *God, Freedom and Evil.* Translation Desidério Murcho. São Paulo: New Life, 2012.

52. RAYMOND, Robert L. *Systematic* theology: part 1 and 2. Amazon e-book.

53. RYRIE, Charles C. Basic theology within the reach of

all. Translation Jarbas Aragon. São Paulo: Editora Mundo Cristão, 2010.

54. SANDERS, J. Oswald. *Paul. the Leader.* Editora Vida, 1986.

55. SCHLESINGER, Hugo. *Jesus was a Jew. Hugo Schlesinger, Humberto Porto. São Paulo: Pauline Editions, 1979.*

56. SCHOPENHAUER, Artur. *The Free Will.* Volume 3 of "The Great Classics of Literature". São Paulo. Novo Brasil, Editora Brasileira Ltda, 1982.

57. SPURGEON, Charles Haddon. Gracious Sermons: 15 Sermons on the Grace of God by the Prince of Preachers. Amazon e-book.

58. WARREN, Rick. *A Life with Purpose.* Editora Vida, 2003.

59. WENHAM, John William. *The Enigma of Evil: Can We Believe in the Goodness of God?* Marcio L. Redondo. São Paulo: New Life, 1989.

60. WILKINSON Michael B. and another. *Philosophy of Religion : an Introduction.* Michael B. Wilkinson, Hugh

N. Capbell. Translation Anoar Jarbas Provenzi. São Paulo. Paulinas, 2014.

61. YANCEY, Philip. *Disappointed in God"*. São Paulo: Editora Vida.

62. YANCEY, Philip. *God (in) visible.* São Paulo: Editora Vida.

63. YANCEY, Philip. *Wonderful Grace.* Translation of Yolanda Krievin. 2nd ed. revised and enlarged. São Paulo: Editora Vida, 2012.

---

[1] 1st Pe 3:15 (BJC).

[2] Ibid.